How to Develop

a Profitable Trade System

Concise Edition

Tony Pow

Contents

Introduction 3
Section 1: Technical Analysis (TA) 6
    1   Technical analysis 7
    2   Examples of using TA 11
    3   Easy TA without charts 16
    4   Bollinger Bands 16
    5   MACD 18
    6   Other TA indicators/patterns 18
    7   More on technical analysis 20
    8   Using Fidelity 21
    9   Simplest market timing 22
Section 2: Momentum investing 25
    1   My momentum performance 31
    2   Four strategies for momentum 34
    3   Herd theory 37
    4   Simplest ways to evaluate stocks 38
Section 3: Simple techniques 42
    1   Quick analysis of ETFs 42
    2   An example 46
    3   Rotate four ETFs 47
    4   The best strategy 49
Appendix 1 – All my books 50
Appendix 2 – Art of Investing 52
Appendix 3 - Our window to the investing world 56
Appendix 4 - ETFs / Mutual Funds 58

Introduction

You need a trading system (same as strategy) to make money for trading for a few stocks or hundreds of stocks a year. It will give you rules to enter a trade and to close a trade. In addition, it gives you suggestions to monitor your trades and how to protect your portfolio.

The trading system can be tailored to your requirements and objectives. This book concentrates on using Technical Analysis.

How to use this book

Most graphs and tables are in landscape orientation (recommended for small screens) for both paperback and e-readers. Some graphs may not be displayed adequately on a small screen of an e-reader. Use PC to read the graphs on the larger screen. For better orientation, just flip your e-reader device 90 degrees if it is available. Most e-readers let you select a table or a graph to display it to fit the screen.

A link is usually included for the most screens. Copy it to your browser to display the graphs on your PC if desirable.

The **font size** (Ctrl Minus for browser implementation of e-readers) should be adjustable.

There are clickable links to web articles. Most of them are from my own web sites and public web sites such as Wikipedia. Some public links may not be available in the future as they are not under my control and my book may change.

These links extend the usefulness of this book by making available specific topics that may not be interesting to every reader. It also provides articles (most are not written by me) for more in-depth analysis.

Fidelity provides video clips to explain some of the basic terms. Fidelity does not require a balance to open an account; I have no affiliation with them except I retired from Fidelity. Take advantage of their extensive research and info. YouTube offers similar video lessons. This book provides many of the links for the paperback readers. In any case, get the same information or extra information by entering a search in Wikipedia and/or Investopedia (http://www.investopedia.com/) such as "Dogs of the Dow".

'Afterthoughts' includes my additional comments and ideas of minor importance. There are fillers with tips, refreshing pictures (taken by me) and jokes (most original) to fill up some empty space of the printed book. Fillers, links and afterthoughts should not disrupt the flow of reading this book. So far, no one has asked me to take them out yet; many readers enjoy them and many treat them as breaks of reading this book.

For convenience, this book uses SPY, an Exchange Traded Fund (ETF) simulating the S&P 500, as the benchmark for the market. Annualized returns (Return * 365 / (Days between)) are used where appropriate for a more meaningful comparison. To illustrate, I had a 10% return in 6 months, a 10% in a year and a 10% in 2 years. It is more meaningful to use annualized returns of 20%, 10% and 5% respectively for the 6-month return, I use one-year return and the 2-year return in this example. Usually I do not include the dividend, so you can add an estimated 1.5% to the annualized return for SPY. In addition, compound interest is not used for easier calculation, so the actual return could be even better.

Since most of the stock recommendations are probably obsolete by the time you read about them, use them as examples and do not trade the mentioned stocks without consulting your financial advisor first. For simplicity, I treat ETN the same as ETF.

About the author

I graduated from Cal. State University at San Jose in Industrial Engineering and the University of Massachusetts in Amherst with a MS in Industrial Engineering. I have retired from a job in IT. I have been an investor for over 30 years and have written over 30 books on investing. Here is the link to some of the articles I have written.

Dedication

To all retail investors and future retail investors including my grandchildren.

Acknowledgement

Thanks to Seeking Alpha, Wikipedia and Investopedia for the many helpful links to enrich this book. Fidelity.com, Yahoo!Finance and Finviz.com for the tools and charts used in this book.

Important notices

© 2020-2022 Tony Pow

Version	
Initial	09/20
1.1	01/21
1.2	04/22

No part of this book can be reproduced in any form without the written approval of the author. My email address is pow_tony@yahoo.com.

Book store managers can order this book from Createspace.com.
https://tonyp4idea.blogspot.com/2020/12/book-managers.html

Book update.
https://ebmyth.blogspot.com/2020/12/updates-for-all-books.html

If this book is thinly sized, imagine how the Kindle version of "Complete the art of investing" with about 850 pages (6*9) would help you financially. That could be the best $10 you invest in.

Disclaimer
Do not gamble with money that you cannot afford to lose. Past performance is a guideline and is not necessarily indicative of future results. All information is believed to be accurate, but there is not a guarantee. All the strategies including charts to detect market plunges described have no guarantee that they will make money and they may lose money. Do not trade without doing due diligence and be warned that most data may be obsolete. All my articles and the associated data are for informational and illustration purposes only. I'm not a professional investment counselor, a tax professional or any other field. Seek one before you make any investment decisions. Remember to consult with a registered financial adviser before making any investment decisions. The above mentioned also applies for all other advice such as on accounting, taxes, health and any topic mentioned in this book. Tax laws change all the time, so talk to your tax advisors before taking any action. Some articles may offend some one or some organization unintentionally. If I did, I'm sorry about that. I am politically and religiously neutral. I have provided my best efforts to ensure the accuracy of my articles. Data also from different sources was believed to be accurate. However, there is no guarantee that they are accurate and suitable for the current market conditions and /or your individual situations. The values of some parameters such as RSI(14) are arbitrarily set by me. I have made a lot of predictions that may not materialize. My publisher and I are not liable for any damages in using this book or its contents.

Section 1: Technical Analysis (TA)

Technical analysis (TA) is the analysis of the price movements and the short-term trend and possible reversal, while fundamental analysis focuses on metrics such as price/earnings ratio and debts. TA assumes the future stock price behavior can be determined by the patterns of past price behavior – it is true more times than untrue. Traders use TA a lot and can profit by shorting stocks. Investors can use them to find the entry points and exits points and some investors only buys stocks with positive long-term trend (using SMA-200%).

Many times stock analysis based on fundamentals fail when the evaluation is solely based on fundamentals. Technical Analysis (TA) has the following characteristics:

- Most of the time, TA is profitable in the short term (less than 3 months). The weather man is more accurate in tomorrow's weather rather than a month away. TA can also signal the reversals.
- It is too many signals if you have more than three TA parameters. To start, use SMA (Simple Moving Average) and RSI(14); both are available in Finviz.com without charting.
- You can combine TA with fundamentals such as a rising SMA50 with increasing Insider Purchases. In addition, you can use more than one TA indictors.
- For market timing, TA is a huge part, but many fundamentals should be considered too. You can use similar techniques to time the market and time stocks and/or sectors such as Golden Cross / Death Cross.

Technical analysis wins for the following reasons:
- Information such as a new product or a major lawsuit pending is not reflected timely in fundamentals, but rather in technical analysis. It gives us guidance in understanding the trend of a stock or even the entire market.
- Most TAs are based on accumulated data. For example, if RSI(14) is greater than 65, most likely this stock is overbought. If there is no reason for this condition, you may consider to sell it.
- When too many investors follow TA, it would become self-prophecy.
- Do not act against the trend. The fundamentalist may buy a stock when it loses 50%, the TA investor most likely will not buy it. Many times the losing stocks will lose another 25% or so. The TA investor most likely buys it on the way up only or short it on the way down.

An example. NVRO (a stock symbol) has appreciated about 100% from mid Feb. to Oct. in 2016 despite its poor fundamentals. It has a new product that could revolutionize physical healing and eliminating pain that will not be shown in the fundamentals except by the eventual Forward P/E. Technical chart can inform us of the uptrend.

Volume is the confirmation. Institution investors drive the market. When the market (esp. the S&P 500 stocks) is down and the volume is up, there is a good chance institution investors are dumping their holdings. It is obvious when most of the indicators are promising but the volume is small.

1   Technical analysis

The basics

Technical analysis (a.k.a. charting) is easier to learn than you might expect. It represents the trend of the market (a stock or a group of stocks) graphically. If more investors are in the market, the market would move upwards until it changes direction. We divide the trends into short-term, intermediate-term and long-term.

The chartists usually do not consider fundamentals as they believe they have already been priced into the stock price and some fundamentals are not available to the public. To illustrate, a new drug has been discovered, the stock price of the company jumps initially by insiders purchases and the informed. Its fundamental metrics do not demonstrate this right away, but many investors are buying to boost up the stock price as evidenced by the technical indicators such as SMA for 20 or 50 days.

The volume is a confirmation. When the stock moves up or down by 10% with a low volume, the trend is not yet confirmed.

The trend of the stock price is not a straight line in most cases. Hence a trend line is usually drawn to indicate the direction of the stock. Many investors believe the stocks fluctuate in certain ranges (i.e. channels) and the chart draws the upper value (the resistance line) and the lower value (the support line). In theory, the price of a stock fluctuates within the resistance line (ceiling for understanding) and support (floor). When it reaches its support, it becomes a buy and vice versa for a sell. Most charts including Finviz.com would display these lines.

When the price passes out of the channel, it is called a breakout. Darvas, one of the oldest and most successful chartists, profited from the breakouts of the resistance line and believed the stock was close to the support line of the new channel. Hence it would be a long way up in theory.

If it were so simple, there will be no poor folks

It works most of the time, but do not place all your money on it. For chartists, 51% is great (the same for playing Black Jack). Some trends reverse very fast such as the bio drug stocks in 2015. You need to hedge your bets such as placing stop orders. Most do not want to spend their lives in watching the trend from a big screen.

Most novices use too many technical indicators and lose in their performances to the professionals. Recently, most chartists were not doing all that great and I did not find many books on their success than a decade ago. It could be due to too many followers in similar setups. I verified it with my recent testing using Finviz.com.

Simple Moving Average

The basic technical indicator is SMA-N. It is the average of the last N trade sessions. When N is 20 (or SMA-20), we classify it as short-term. Similarly, SMA-50 is an intermediate-term and SMA-200 is long-term. I prefer 50, 100 and 250. This trend duration is important. For example, do not want to place long-term purchases using the short-term SMA-50. There are many modifications to SMA such as giving more weight to recent data, but I have not found them any better. Finviz.com includes this information without charting (SMA-20, SMA-50 and SMA-100 in percentages).

Defining the trend periods is rather arbitrary. I use SMA-350 to detect the market plunges and SMA-100 for stocks. Weighted Moving Average weighs more weight on recent price data.

The trend is your best friend
Most traders use TA for trending in a short duration. Investors can also use TA to time the entry and exit points for better potential profits. Value investors usually are patient and they do bottom fishing and they search for 'oversold' condition using RSI(14). Again high volume is a confirmation.

Many sites provide charting free of charge such as Yahoo!Finance. Finviz.com provides a lot of technical indicators without charting such as

SMA% and RSI(14). It also provides screen searching for stocks that meet your technical analysis criteria.

Hands on
Bring up Finviz.com and enter any stock symbol such as AAPL. You can see the daily prices of AAPL from about nine months ago to today. Three SMAs (Simple Moving Average) are displayed as SMA-20, SMA-50 and SMA-200. The first two are for short-term trends. When the price is above the SMA, it is expected to be trending up. Again, the trade volume is used as a confirmation.

You can also see the resistance line and the support line drawn. In theory, the stock will trade within these lines. When it exceeds its resistance line, it is called a breakout, and vice versa for a breakdown. Sometimes it displays some technical patterns such as Cup and Shoulder and Double Down (both are positive patterns).

Select Weekly data. The Candle chart is better described than the Daily chart. Candles give us better descriptions of the price: open, close, high and low. The green color indicates the price is up for the period (a week in this example) and the red color indicates a down period.

In addition, Finviz.com includes some technical indicators in the metric section such as RSI. Most other chart sites are similar in the basics. Use Finviz's Help and select Technical Analysis for more description. Investopedia has enhanced descriptions on this topic.

TA patterns

There are many TA patterns such as Bollinger Bands and MACD. The patterns are based on the stock prices and many times they prove to be correct predictions especially on stocks with high volume and high market caps. Patterns have been repeating themselves many times as they are driven by investors.

Sites for TA
There are many free sites for charts with explanations of their technical indicators. Popular ones include BigCharts.com, SmallCharts.com and Yahoo!Finance. Fidelity includes some unique features in its charts such as P/E.

Why I do not use TA as a primary tool for stock picking

My investing style is different from a day trader's. I prefer to 'Buy Low and Sell High' instead of 'Buy High and Sell Higher'. I try to find the real bottom price. TA will not find the bottom very easily but it tracks the trend better. As a bargain hunter, I do not expect the stock will rise fast as I'm usually swimming against the tide. However, value stocks could stay in the low price for a long time (i.e. value trap). I like to select stocks that turn around as evidenced by the SMA-20 and SMA-50.

With that said, my momentum portfolio has appreciated consistently and usually has the best performing stocks among all my portfolios. It is based on the timely grade from my subscriptions plus the metrics on timing.

Most chartists would also tell you to buy the stocks that have broken out (i.e. higher than the resistance line) and/or stocks at their highs. Contrary to value investing, you should exit when the trend reverses. The reversal could happen very fast and hence protect your portfolio by setting up stop loss (preferably with trailing stop) orders.

My opinion

I do not want to argue whether TA is good for you or not. You need to find that out. Most likely, the day traders and very short-term traders will profit more from TA than the investors seeking value stocks for the long-term gains.

Random remarks

Even if you do not use technical analysis, you should spend some time in learning it. It is better to marry fundamentals and TA. My random remarks are:

- The Institutional investors (insurance companies, pension funds, mutual funds, etc.) use TA and they MOVE the market. A lot of times it becomes a self-fulfilling prophecy. It is better to join them as most of us cannot beat them.
- Day traders take advantage of the institutional investors by spotting their trends.
- Most TA stocks should be good sized and have large average daily volumes. I prefer to use TA on value stocks to prevent long-term losses.
- I do know some folks making big money using TA, but I know more making good money using fundamentals. Since TA predicts the market

- better in the shorter term, its practitioners may have to pay higher taxes (in today's tax laws) in taxable accounts.
- Our objective should be making money with the least risk. Once you claim to belong to a certain group of either Fundamental or TA, you will be biased and forget your primary objective in investing.
- TA tracks the last two big market plunges (2000 and 2007) pretty well. The chart will not warn you right away for the upcoming plunge (as it depends on past data) to avoid the initial losses, but they will warn you to avoid bigger losses.

Afterthoughts

- Besides searching for stocks that have potential breakouts, we should check the stocks we owned for potential breakdowns.
  Technical Analysis tutorial.
  https://www.YouTube.com/watch?v=GENBVwV8PMs

  SMA tutorial.
  https://www.YouTube.com/watch?v=Na-ctpPsnks

Links

Fidelity video: Technical Analysis
https://www.fidelity.com/learning-center/technical-analysis/chart-types-video

2   Examples of using TA

I have outlined how we can spot market plunges using TA and I use it to monitor the market every three months or so (I recommend to do it every month and even more frequently when the market is risky). Here is an example of how to use it to trade individual stocks.

I have to admit I do not use TA that much on individual stocks and clearly I am not an expert in TA. If this article stirs up your interest, read more books or attend seminars / classes on TA. However, this book describes the basic and most useful technical indicators. There are many good and free articles from Investopedia on this topic. Personally I prefer to seek fundamentally sound companies at bargain prices and wait for their full appreciation. It has been proven to me many times over.

TA is very useful for momentum and day traders. With the rising volume, you can detect that the stocks are traded by managers of mutual funds, hedge funds, insurance companies and pension funds, and you profit by riding on their wagons.

Some stocks are good for TA. Usually they are larger companies with above-average volumes and are fundamentally sound. Avoid the stocks that are trending downwards unless you're bottom fishing. Let me pick CSCO (a cyclical stock) for an illustration. I bought it several times in 2012. I sold some in 2013 and 2014 making good profits. This is quite different from what short-term traders would use during the following:

The green line is a 50-day simple moving average (SMA) for the following chart using one year data.

If it does not display clearly on a small screen, type the following on the browser in your PC.

http://ebmyth.blogspot.com/2013/05/chart-for-ta-example.html

Buy the stock when it is above its SMA and sell when it is below. Following the chart would make good money based on this simple rule. Also, practice the strategy "Sell on May 1, Buy back on Nov. 1".

Not all stocks follow this profitable pattern. Fundamentalists may try to pick the bottom in late July while chartists enter positions on its upward trend. The chartists have an advantage to stay away from stocks in their downward trend.

Exponential Moving Average has better predictable power as it weighs more on recent prices. Some indicators / patterns work better in specific market conditions – all markets are different.

Volume is important as a confirmation. If the price of a stock is up with thin volume, the rise is questionable and it could be manipulated.

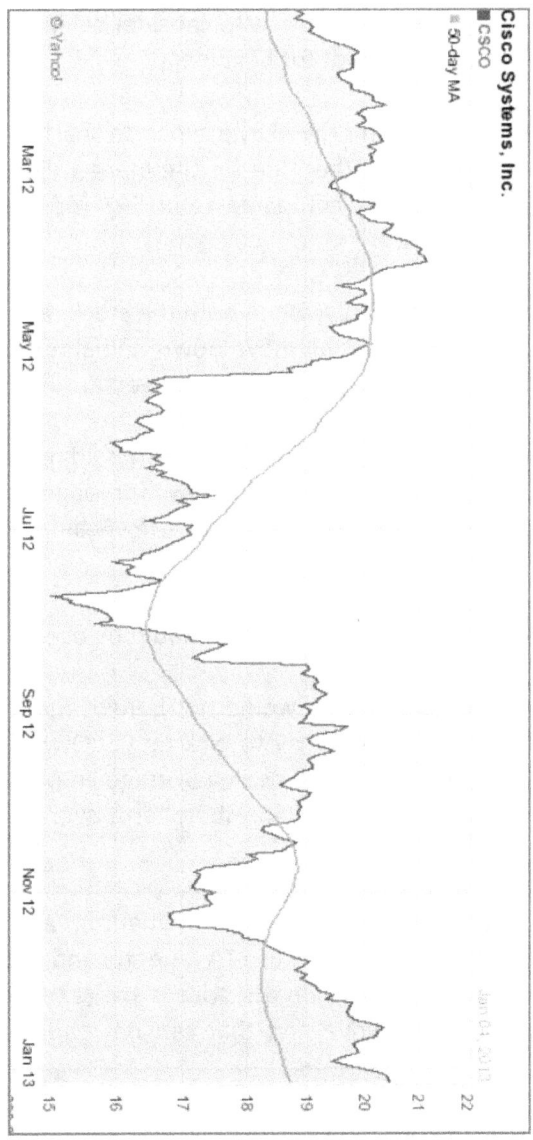

Table: CSCO 50-day SMA   Source: Yahoo!Finance

We can improve the trades by:
- Use different moving average in the number of days (50 in this example) and other indicators such as EMA (a moving average that weighs higher on more recent data). It may improve prediction accuracy and/or cut down on the number of trades. RSI(14) suggests overbought / oversold conditions.

- Instead of selling the stock for cash, consider selling the stock short. Selling short is definitely not for beginners.

- The accuracy is usually improved by a separate chart for the sector the stock belongs to and another one for the market. For CSCO, you can use an ETF for network companies and SPY (or a similar ETF) to represent the market.

  In theory and in theory only, when both the stock, the sector that the stock is in and the market all move down, the stock price has a high chance that it would move down, and vice versa.

  We use the 50 days (in SMA) for short-term holding of stocks (20 for even shorter holding period and 200 days for longer holding period). Personally I use 30 days for the sector ETF. Again, 'Days' is actually 'Trade Sessions'.

TA is not for most fundamentalists but it should be used

For a bargain hunter like me, TA would not benefit me a lot for picking stocks at their bottoms. I would try to pick up CSCO with prices ranging from 15-17 and all well below the moving average line, but TA would not show me a Buy signal. However, for short-term swing traders TA is a Godsend.

To me, TA is a good indicator for growth, momentum and for short-term trading. Some fundamentalists may use TA for entry and exit point is. Some recommend buying the stock when the price is above the SMA-200 (same as when SMA-200% is positive and that can be readily obtained from Finviz.com).

It is profitable for 'Buy High and Sell Higher' if you can are able to protect your profits effectively. This is also called 'Buy at a reasonable cost'. One's opinion.

In selecting a tool, you have to understand how, and why to use it and whether it fits your investing style. I use TA for market timing for the entire market more than on individual stocks. When I have more time, I probably would use TA more frequently.

Most of us cannot spot the bottom of a stock; I have had some success but most likely they were due to luck. When a stock is moving up from the bottom, there is a good chance it will move further up. TA shows it and the volume confirms it.

Conclusion

Even a fundamentalist like me can benefit a lot by using TA. This book touches on the very basics of TA.

Besides monitoring the fundamentals of the stocks you bought once every 6 months, you should analyze their technical indicators more often (1 month to 3 months depending on your available time). When the market is risky (close to the SMA average), run the SMA chart more frequently (say once a week).

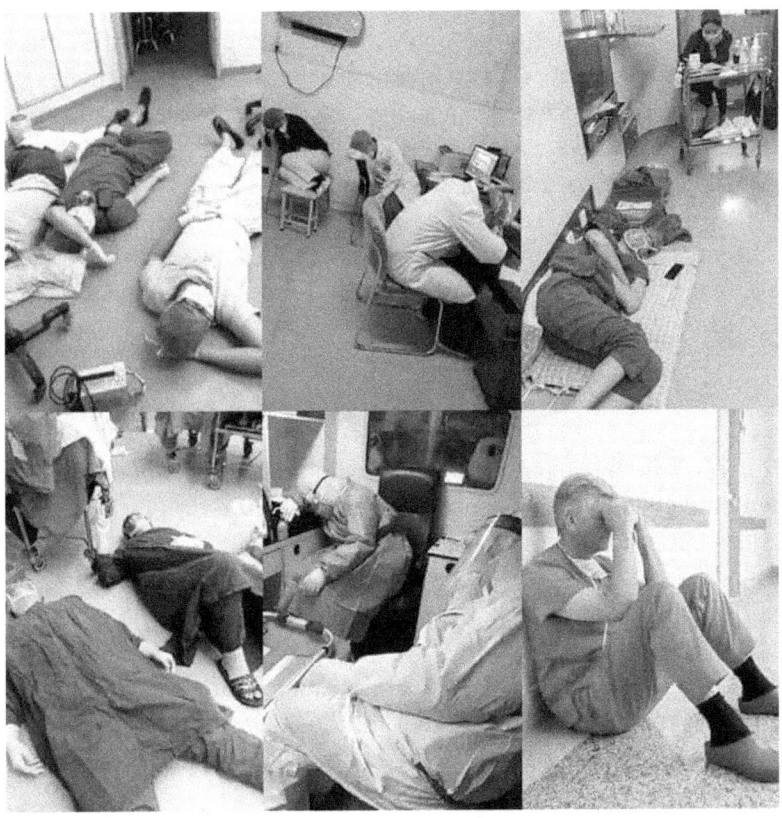

Not taken by me.
They are more important than ALL entertainers and athletes

3 Easy TA without charts

Bring up Finviz.com from your browser. Enter the stock you're evaluating. SMA-200% stands for Simple Moving Average of the last 200 trade sessions. RSI(14)% is the relative strength index for the last 14 trade sessions.

The following is just a suggestion with conservative parameters. Adjust the parameters according to your risk tolerance and requirements. Do not buy the stock with SMA-200% is < 0 (trending down), SMA-200% > 40 (peaking), or RSI(14)% > 65 (overbought).

Filler: Love is blind

The dividend lovers say that when their stocks drop by 50%, they are getting a 50% raise. There was a recent article on this STUPID logic - insulting my intelligence by just reading the title. When the company is bankrupted, they are getting a 100% raise. Should they check in the closest clinic to get their brains examined?

Love is blind and fools are fools and this cannot change the truths in our lives.

---

4 Bollinger Bands

Bollinger Bands have been proven useful for traders. In theory, the stock is traded between the upper band and the lower band forming an envelope. For more info, click the following link.

http://www.investopedia.com/terms/b/bollingerbands.asp

The following chart was drawn by Yahoo!Finance for CSCO from 8/7/2012 to 8/7/2014 selecting Bollinger Bands for the 50 days as a parameter. If you trade more often, use 20 days. If the chart is too small to display on your screen, enter the following in your PC's browser.
http://ebmyth.blogspot.com/2014/08/screen-csco-bollinger-bands-50.html

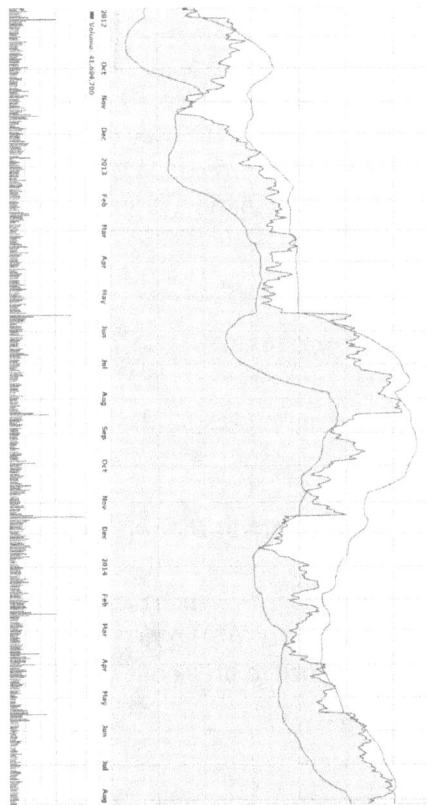

Bollinger Bands 50 Days.   Source: Yahoo!Finance

You buy the stock when the price is close to the lower band and sell the stock when it is close to the upper band.

When the stock price passes the upper band, it is called a breakout. Similar for the stock falling below the lower band.

From the above, we should make some good money.

It is advisable to use at least one more technical indicator. I recommend the RSI(14), which is also accessible from Yahoo!Finance or similar sites. When it is above 70, it is overbought, so I recommend selling the stock. When it is below 30, it is oversold, so I recommend buying the stock. However, fundamentals have not been considered. Some stocks just go to zero and some just surge.

5   MACD

MACD, Moving Average Convergence Divergence, is an effective momentum (i.e. short-term) indicator used by most traders. When the stock price is crossing above the zero line, it is a buy and vice versa. It may give false signals in sideways fluctuation.

---

6   Other TA indicators/patterns

They are briefly mentioned here. Click on the links or use Investopedia for more descriptions.

Double Bottom is a bullish pattern as the support line is stronger than the resistance line.
Double Top is the opposite and is a bearish pattern. I prefer the price of the second top is less than the price of the first top. It seems there are no enough investment in this stock to break out of the second top.

Resistance and Support. The stock is supposed to fluctuate between an imaginary zone of resistance and support. Short-term traders may sell when the price is close to the resistance line and close any short positions when it is close to the support line. However, breakouts from this zone are possible and many traders trade stocks on breakouts. It is a little similar to 52-week highs and lows. The trend line indicates the trend of the stock.

Cup and handle is a bullish pattern. The stock price peaks and then forms a shape of a cup and handle.

Head & Shoulder is a bearish pattern while the reversed Head & Shoulder is a bullish pattern. It signals that the peak (the head) has been reached and the second top (the shoulder) has failed to reach the previous peak.

Stochastic Oscillator. It is similar to RSI(14). Many traders use this indicator. If it is above 65, it is overbought. If it is below 30, it is oversold. In general, I would trade on an uptrend when the stock is moving from 60 to 85; it depends on how volatile the stock is. It is better to use with other indicators and as a reference.

To illustrate when to buy, one suggestion is to buy when this indicator changes to an uptrend while the price is still going down.

Many traders follow these technical indicators and SMA. They could become "self-fulfilled" prophecies.

Link

Chart patterns. https://www.youtube.com/watch?v=o6hZma0bajE

###

Again, try to master SMA and RSI(14) first. Using too many indicators usually harms you more than helps you. You can use Finviz.com to search stocks with technical indicators.

7 More on technical analysis

This chapter describes some TA indicators that can help us. Click on the following links for a better description.

- Finviz.com.
  It has SMA20%, SMA50% and SMA200% to represent the short-term, intermediate-term and the long-term indicator. SMA stands for Simple Moving Average and n for days for the duration of the average (for example, 20 days for SMA20%).

  If you are a long-term investor, use SMA-200% (or SMA-350%). Using SMA-20% would cause a lot of sells / reentries, which costs more in trading fees.

  Buy when the price is above the Moving Average line and sell when the price is below it. Finviz.com provides the percent of moving above the moving average to indicate just how much the price deviates from the average.

  If you hold the stock for an average of 50 days, use SMA50%, and so on. If you hold stocks for an average of 90 days, you have to create your own SMA using one of the many web sites including Yahoo!Finance and specify 90 days for the period.

  Try other similar technical indicators such as EMA, which is supposed to weigh more on the more recent data. A weather man can predict tomorrow's weather better than the weather a week away.

- RSI(14) indicates whether the stock is overbought or oversold. RSI oscillates between zero and 100. Traditionally, and according to Wilder (the author of this method), RSI is considered overbought with a value above 70 and oversold with a value below 30 as described in the article.

  When it is oversold, most likely the stock will fall, and vice versa.

(http://stockcharts.com/school/doku.php?id=chart_school:technical_indicators:relative_strength_index_rsi)

   Click here for another article.
(http://financial-dictionary.thefreedictionary.com/Relative+Strength+Index)

- Cup and handle is a popular indicator of when the stock price would surge.
  (http://www.investopedia.com/terms/c/cupandhandle.asp)

- Double bottom indicates that the stock will move up.
  (http://stockcharts.com/school/doku.php?id=chart_school:chart_analysis:chart_patterns:double_bottom_revers)

  It shows a double bottom for Apple in 2013.

8   Using Fidelity

Click "Research and News" and then "Stock". Simple charting and advanced charting are both provided.

Hints:
- Fidelity provides suggested stops.
- Click on the Support and Resistance under Technical Analysis to display the Resistance Line (upper limit). Click on the Resistance Line and you can get the Support Line (lower limit).
- Click on Advanced Chart and then click on "learn how to use the chart".
- Under Advanced Chart, select Draw and Trend Line. Select the upper line by touching the highest points and do the same for the lower line.

9 Simplest market timing

Why market timing
Before 2000, market timing was a waste of time. However, after that, we have had two market plunges with the average loss of about 45%. It sounds harder to time the market than it actually is. We have a simple technique to detect market plunges and when to reenter the market. Our objective is reducing the loss to 25%.

Market timing depends on charts; the following describes how to use chart information without creating charts. Most charts will not identify the peaks and bottoms of the market as they depend on data (i.e., the stock prices). However, it would reduce further losses. It is simpler than it sounds. Just follow the procedure below.

The first part of this technique detects potential market plunges, and the second part advises you when to start reentering the market. It applies to individual stocks too. It also works to detect the trend of a sector (entering an ETF for the specific sector instead of SPY) and a specific stock.

Step-by-step procedure
When the market timer indicator (Death Cross) described next tells you to exit the market, sell SPY (an ETF simulating S&P 500). Do not forget to buy back SPY or similar ETF such as RSP, when the indicator (Golden Cross) tells you to return.

My experiences in 2000s
Basically I did the same as the above with some adaptations. I worked for a mutual fund company and they did not allow me to trade stocks effectively. However, I was allowed to trade sector funds offered by the company. Every two months, I switched to the sectors with the best performances for the last month. When most sectors were down for the last month, I rotated them to the money market fund. In March or April, 2000, I switched to traditional sectors from high-tech sectors (better to switch to market money fund). During the time, I bought those stocks that had cash enough to last more than two years judging by their burn rates. The indicators should do a better job.

How to detect market plunges without charts (similar to Death Cross)
1. Bring up Finviz.com.
2. Enter SPY (or any ETF that simulates the market) or RSP for equally weighed SPY.

3. If SMA-200% is positive, it indicates that the market plunge has not been detected and you can skip the following steps.
4. The market is plunging if SMA-50% is more negative than SMA-200%. To illustrate this condition, SMA-200% is -2% and SMA-50% is -5%.
5. Conservative investors should sell most stocks starting with the riskiest ones first such as the ones with negative earnings, high P/Es and/or high Debt/Equity. Obtain this info from Finviz.com by entering the symbol of the stock you own.
6. Aggressive investors should sell all stocks. Extremely aggressive investors should sell all stocks, buy contra ETFs, and even short stocks. I do not recommend beginners to be aggressive.

Example
As of 2/12/2022, the following are from Finviz.com.

ETF	SMA-200	SMA-50	SMA-20	Death Cross?
SPY	-0.8%	-4.2%	-1.7%	Yes (Step #4)
RSP	-0.5%	-1.9%	0.4%	Yes (Step #4)

Both ETFs indicate the market is a confirmed crash from my indications using a technique similar to Death Cross. However, they are quite close, and we should keep an eye on these numbers. In this case, SMA-20 has not been used. If it is a false alarm, the Golden Cross would indicate it and you should return to equity; it could be quite common in volatile markets. The futures indicate that on Monday (2/14/22) the market would plunge further.

Another test is using SMA-350: When the current price is below SMA-300, it is a crash. SMA-20 has to be more negative than SMA-50 and it has not been used here.

When to return to the market (similar to Golden Cross)

Use the above in a reversed sense to detect whether the market has been recovering. However, when the SMA-200% turns positive, I would start buying value stocks (low P/E but the 'E' has to be positive, and/or low Debt/Equity).

1. Bring up Finviz.com.
2. Enter SPY (or any ETF that simulates the market).
3. If SMA-200% is negative, the market is not recovering, and you can skip the following steps.
4. Sell all contra ETFs and close all shorts if you have any.
5. Market recovery is confirmed when SMA-50% is more positive than SMA-200%. To illustrate this condition, SMA-200% is 2% and SMA-50% is 5%.

Commit a large percent of cash (or all cash for aggressive investors) to stocks. If you do not know what to buy, buy SPY or an ETF that simulates the market.

How often should you check the market timing indicators?

Do the above once a month. When the SPY price is closer to SMA actions percentage, perform the above once a week. The charts and data for market timing described in this book are based on SMA-350 (Simple Moving Average) that is more preferable than this simple procedure, but it requires some simple charting.

Nothing is perfect

If the market timing is perfect, there would be no poor folks. The major 'defects' are:
- It does not detect the peak / bottom as it depends on past data. However, it would save you a lot during the crash.
- It is hard to determine whether it is a correction or a crash.
- From 2000 to 2010, there was only one false signal. The indicator tells you to exit and then tells you to reenter the market shortly. In most cases, you do not lose a lot. After 2010, we have more false signals.
- The market may not be rational or may be influenced due to specific conditions such as excessive printing of USD. If you do not mind charting, use SMA 350 (or 400) using SPY. Buy when the price is above SMA-350 (or SMA-400), and sell otherwise. SMA-400 reduces the number of false signals, but it is not nimble.

#Filler: Glad to be an investor

After watching the following YouTube video, I am glad my parents did not push me to play piano and also glad I do not have any musical gene. How can I compete with this kid?

https://www.youtube.com/watch?v=yf0B4rVoq44

Also, glad not into some life-threatening professions such as surgical doctors, soldiers, fire fighters, etc. I can make mistakes in investing from time to time without suffering from the consequences. With the uptrend market for most of the last 50 years, most investors should make good money. Thank God.

Section 2: Momentum investing

This strategy provides me with steady income by working an hour or two every week. How long will it last? I do not know. I will describe the concept here, so you can devise your own to fit your risk tolerance and requirements.

As of this writing, this strategy is having amazing returns. Though these returns may not be sustainable, my convictions are so strong that I am boldly increasing my investment. When the market is trending up, this strategy is very profitable particularly if the stocks are in the rising sectors. When the market is trending down, find the worst stocks and short them.

The concept of a momentum strategy

Each week, I buy about 5 stocks based on the momentum metrics and sell them within a month. I do not use the fundamental metrics a lot, as that will not be effective in such a short duration. From my current record, the average holding time is about 20 days.

The details of my strategy will not be disclosed fully but the concept is. When a strategy is used too often, it will not be effective and would end up churning the same stocks for all its followers. However, let me elaborate on the implementation of this momentum strategy and give you some ideas on how to build one for yourself.

My Theory. When a stock is on the uptrend, most likely it will continue for at least for a week or two. Do not buy stocks when the market is risky. Protect yourself by using stops and / or using technical indicators such as SMA-20 (Simple Moving Average).

Subscription services

I spend less than half an hour to find about 6 stocks to buy. My choice is helped by subscription services. Some have earnings revision information (particularly useful during earnings seasons) and most others have provided timing grades. I include the insider purchase information and short-term technical indicators. It works so far and I constantly monitor the performance.

For starters, use simple screens and procedures to find stocks without getting a subscription service. Paper trade your screens and strategies to include your average holding period and money management before you commit to use real money.

Common parameters

I subscribe to several investment services and select their recommendations. From my recent reviews, I only need a good subscription with historical database plus the free Fidelity, Yahoo!Finance and Finviz. Most of these sites provide a timing ranking. The rank for value should take a back seat in momentum stocks.

To illustrate, the composite rank for timing in Blue Chip Growth (not free any more) is the Quantitative Score. It is also known as the buying pressure. Fidelity provides similar rankings.

http://navelliergrowth.investorplace.com/bluechip/password/index.php?plocation=%2Fbluechip%2F.

There are several common parameters on how they rank stocks. These parameters may be obtained from Finviz.com.

- Price momentum. I prefer to use SMA20% (20-day simple moving average). The higher the percentage, the better. However, they should not be too high (say greater than 15%). When it is peaking, the stock may fall.

- Change of short %. Favorable if it is over 25% (for short squeezes) and unfavorable if it is moving up (say from 5% to 15%). You need to keep track of the previous short percentages for the stocks you follow.

- Sales momentum (Sales Q/Q) and earnings momentum (EPS Q/Q or quarter earnings to quarter prior year). The higher, the better.

- Earnings revisions. Zacks (free for a single stock) has good info based on their estimates and rumors.

- Insider's Purchase. No one knows the company better than its officers. You can find the Insider Transaction from Finviz.

- Analysts' recommendation. It can be obtained from Finviz.com. However, Fidelity's Equity Summary Score provides a better one and it is based on the past performances of the analysts' predictions.

Reduce Taxes

I use my Roth accounts to minimize my taxes. There are many tax advantages of a Roth account. The second choice is other retirement accounts. I converted some of my Roll-over IRA to my Roth as allowed. Consult your tax lawyer or CPS for updated information about your individual situations.

Reduce losses during market downfall

My strategy works best in the up market as I seldom short stocks. However, a major market downfall could wipe out all profits for years. In 2019, I was shorting stocks more often as the market was risky.

These are two Technical Analysis tools to anticipate a market downfall. Minimize losses once a downfall of the market has been spotted.

- Do not buy any stock.

- Sell any existing positions and/or use stops to reduce further losses.

- Aggressive investors should buy contra ETFs such as DOG, SH and PSQ (against the corresponding indexes DOW, the S&P500 and NASDAQ) when the market is too risky. It is like buying insurance (hedging your portfolio). However, do not be the entire farm.

- Be disciplined. Most likely, your strategy should be profitable despite its ups and downs of the market especially in the long run.

- Be emotionally detached. As of 4/2013, my average annualized return of 66 round-trip trades was 127%. It is so far so good, but it will not be sustainable in the longer run. I do expect some losses.

- Take a break from time to time. I have stopped this strategy for a while due to the risky market and taking a long vacation.

Monitor performance

I constantly monitor my metrics and my screens for performance. I am always looking at perfecting better systems and /or adapting to the current market conditions.

- Day of the week.
  Monday is not a good day to find stocks. Most of my subscriptions do not update their information on weekends, and the prices are the same as last Friday. I try not to trade on Fridays as I hate to leave unexecuted orders over the weekend.

- Reduce the number of stocks.
  Usually I have an average of eight stocks for further analysis each time, and I select the five stocks or less after evaluation.

- Listen to the experts.
  If all the timing grades from different subscription services are high for a specific stock, the appreciation potential of this stock should be high

- Maximize profit.
  If this strategy proves itself and the market is not risky, I'll increase my position and vice versa.

- Improve performance and reduce risk.
  I have found that about 10% of the gains were due to good timing. If the purchased stock appreciates more than my target price, I sell it right away. My average holding period in this period is about 20 days and the gain is about 3% (the annualized return is huge due to the short average duration).

  From my limited data so far, holding stocks for 20 days gives them better performance rather than holding them longer than 60 days.

- Calculating the rate of return.
  I prefer the annualized rate of return for a better comparison. However, I would skip using those performances from trades with the holding period less than five days. I also compare my return to the return of S&P 500 on the same holding period.

  The better rate to calculate the rate of return is: Total Profit / Total Investment. We have cash between trades. It is too time-consuming for most.

- Money management.
  In a rising market, usually too much idle cash (due to many buy orders are not executed) would decrease the performance of the portfolio and vice versa in a falling market.

In a falling or risky market, limit your stock holding exposure to market risk. Instead of holding the stocks for a month, try to sell them in a week or two, and increase your cash position. You need cash to buy stocks when the market returns.

- If you do not use market orders, try to place the order price as close as the last executed price in the market. I usually submit orders after 10 am; they call the first hour (9:30 am to 10:30 am in NYC) the amateur hour for a good reason.

- My purchase prices are usually about a little less (.2%) than the market prices and sometimes even lower especially when the market is trending downward.

  When the stock is trending up, there is a good chance my purchase order is not executed. I summed up the potential profits lost and the money I saved from the discounts in my purchase prices. It turns out they even each other. In several instances, the stocks just rocket upwards. If I cannot buy the stock after 4 or so hours, I should switch the buy order to market order.

- I prefer to beat the market by smaller margin but more consistently.

- Using a trading plan makes it a discipline and avoids emotional influences.

Recent (4/2016) examples

Recently there were two coaster-roller stocks: Fitbits and GPro. Both stock prices surged through the roof and crashed down. Using "Buy High and Sell Higher" strategy should have made you some money if you protected your profit via trailing stops.

The momentum is caused by the publicity and the public who follow the trend blindly. The fundamentals of both companies when they were rising, they did not justify the prices. It is like buying a hot dog cart in NYC for a million dollar. Of course, you will sell a lot of hot dogs as long as you do not have another hot dog cart next to your cart. However, your investment may never be recouped. In addition, both are single-product companies; it would be very risky when there is competition. Apple is one for Fitbits and I bet many Chinese companies are making products similar to GPro's. GPro's products could be a fad, or they may fall into a limited, specialized market.

Ignore fundamentals for momentum stocks. Ride on the wagon and jump off when the trend reverses.

Afterthoughts

There are several SA articles on similar topic, click here, here and here.

The links are:
http://seekingalpha.com/article/1336291-does-momentum-investing-actually-work?v=1365785958&source=tracking_notify

http://seekingalpha.com/article/865091-how-price-momentum-and-bull-markets-go-together?source=kizur

http://seekingalpha.com/article/1350651-seeking-alpha-momentum-investing-with-etfs

#Filler

Percentage wise, my momentum investing has been most profitable so far. I classify this strategy into 3 sub strategies depending on the average durations.

Filler: Definitions of 'ism'

Capitalism is: You do not work, you die.

Communism is: Everyone is paid the same, so there is no incentive to work harder.

Socialism: As Margaret said, when we have nothing more to give, we all go hungry like the USA is going to.

Idealism: There is no such word in reality. It only exists in our dreams. However, many treat this as it is a reality as they're still dreaming.

Feudalism. Like the Tibetan monks in the 50s. Only the monks can learn and the rest are slaves.

---

1   My momentum performance

The following includes all the actual transactions from September, 2013 to Dec., 2013 in my momentum portfolio. "Lot Date" is the day I evaluate what stocks to buy. Some stocks are bought in different days after the evaluation and some are not bought. I am not responsible for any errors in preparing the following tables.

Lot Date	Stock	Buy Date	Days	Ann. %
09/04/13	BOFI	09/04/13	6	(175%)
	GMCR	09/04/13	14	110%
	Z	09/04/13	6	40%
	FB	09/05/13	8	419%
	AFOP	09/04/13	6	353%
	EGAN	09/04/13	5	194%
	PB	09/06/13	10	78%
09/11/13	ARWR	09/12/13	12	136%
	CATM	09/13/13	4	136%
	GILD	09/13/13	6	157%
	YELP	09/11/13	6	242%
	TRN	09/13/13	32	24%
09/24/13	AFOP	09/26/13	22	(105%)
	DRYS	09/24/13	81	15%
	PACB	09/28/13	20	(258%)
10/02/13	ZLC	10/02/13	14	293%
	FB	10/02/13	15	20%
10/05/13	DYAX	10/08/13	16	(109%)
	FSS	10/08/13	31	160%
10/18/13	GERN	10/18/13	21	1176%
	ALGN	10/22/13	48	(22%)
	COBZ	10/22/13	62	108%
	WAL	10/18/13	21	103%
	LCI	10/22/13	10	434%
	AKRX	10/31/13	15	334%
	BREW	11/01/13	7	194%
	BCEI	10/22/13	10	434%
	RAD	10/22/13	41	142%
11/05/13	LCC merged	11/06/13	3	639%
	TRN	11/08/13	63	41%
	CIR	11/05/13	43	21%
11/12/13	LCI	11/12/13	38	138%
	TRN	11/12/13	3	785%
	UBNT	11/12/13	3	1461%
	LCC	11/12/13	61	20%
	FCN	11/12/13	38	(12%)
11/19/13	FOE	11/19/13	35	(6%)
	NUVA	12/11/13	9	93%
11/25/13	GTN	12/03/13	3	1289%

	CRY	11/26/13	49	39%
	ARC	11/26/13	24	(85%)
	BONT	12/20/13	25	(344%)
12/03/13	AIRM	12/03/13	17	44%
	FIX	12/03/13	20	(97%)
12/10/13	MDXG	12/19/13	8	1162%
	MPAA	12/16/13	7	(7%)
	LBMH	12/14/13	6	627%
	UVE	12/11/13	12	48%
	USAK	12/10/13	13	(18%)
	ARC	12/10/13	13	(144%)
	CONN	12/12/13	11	55%
	REI	12/10/13	10	192%
		Biggest loss		(344%)
		Average		200%

My best profitable month

All the stocks purchased have been sold. Some stocks were bought twice in another account and they may have been in different prices/holding durations. Stopped this strategy in 2019 due to the risky market, but will return when the market is less risky. In 2019, I switched to shorting stocks. Jan., 2014 was one of my best months then.

Lot Date	Stock	Buy Date	Days	Ann. %
01/14/14	LCI	01/14/14	30	85%
	ENDP	01/16/14	42	140%
	LCI	01/14/14	38	208%
	NSTG	01/14/14	56	36%
	BABY	01/26/14	35	156%
	NSTG	01/14/14	59	34%
	ZNGX	01/21/14	31	133%
01/22/14	ANIP	01/22/14	29	195%
	KS	01/22/14	33	115%
	CHIP	01/22/14	19	246%
	SLXP	01/22/14	33	77%
	GMCR	01/22/14	20	743%
		Biggest loss		34%
		Average		181%

Explanation

- Lot Date. I usually group the stocks I buy by weeks. When I have losses two times in a row, I would buy fewer stocks or even skip purchase altogether.

I try to maintain a total balance for this portfolio. I would buy fewer stocks when the balance is close to this threshold. As of 3/15/14, the market is too risky (plunging or peaking), and hence I would not buy any momentum stocks. When the market falls, these momentum stocks will fall faster and steeper than the rest of the market.

- I started this momentum portfolio far earlier, but I only recorded it recently. I took a long summer break in 2013 and resumed it in September, 2013 (the start date of the first table).

  There are some positions not sold after Dec., 2013. Anyway, I have enough data for illustration purposes. Most likely, the reason for showing any 'unclosed' positions is due to housekeeping errors, not trying to present a better result than what may appear.

- I did not include the stocks that have not been bought due to my lower buy prices and/or not meeting my criteria of what to buy. When any of my subscription services tells me the stock is not a buy, I skip it. A few times, some recommended stocks just skyrocketed in prices in the open. I did not buy most if not all of these stocks.

- I've averaged the returns for the above tables. The first table has 200% annualized return while the second one has 181%.

  However, the actual profit of this portfolio is far better in the second table – most likely due to some larger position sizes. The higher annualized return in the first table is due to shorter durations. In my actual monitor, I ignore the returns if they are less than five days, as they distort the returns.

- The actual performance should be worse due to not considering the idle cash. I also exclude the contra ETFs to hedge the portfolio. In 2013, the hedging is a losing game in a rising market. Dividends are not considered in calculating the returns.

- The better way is to compare the performances with the S&P 500 index, which is too time-consuming for me.
- My holding period is short. With many exceptions, I sell these stocks within a month or they have appreciated a lot.
- You can have a portfolio for momentum stocks and another one for value stocks.

2 Four strategies for momentum

We have 3 strategies according to the different holding periods. The screen parameters (i.e. selection criteria) are briefly described here. Adjust them to fit your risk tolerance and requirements. Monitor them from time to time as the market always changes.

Metric	Strategy #1	Strategy #2	Strategy #3
Avg. holding period	< 30 days	60 days	90 days
General			
Market Cap	300 M – 2 B	300 M – 2B	2B – 10B
Avg. volume	>100K	>200K	> 300 K
Analyst Rec[1]	Buy or better	Buy or better	Buy or better
Country	USA	USA	USA
Price	>$5	>$10	>$10
Insider Purchases	Positive	Positive	Positive
Fundamental			
P/E	>0	>0	>0
Forward P/E	>0	>0	>0
Return on Equity		>10%	>10%
EPS Growth next year		>15%	>10%
Technical			
Performance	Week up	Week up	Week up
SMA-20%	> 5%		
SMA-50%	> 0%	>2%	
SMA-200%	>0%	>0%	>0%

[1] I usually do not care about fundamentals for momentum stocks.

In addition, they should be in one of the 3 major exchanges: NYSEX, NASDQA and AMEX (Finviz.com allows you to select one exchange at a time).

In general, Strategy #1 does not care about fundamental. Strategy #2 is a typical sector rotation candidate. Strategy #3 cares more about fundamentals.

I recommend to paper trade your strategy using different selection criteria. When you are comfortable, commit a small amount of cash and increase your portfolio size gradually.

Vendors

Most services charge a fee. However, many free sites provide momentum (same as timing) score. Most have a score (same as rank and grade) for timing. Usually they are based on the momentum of the price. If the price jumps very fast and high, this score is high. Use stops to protect your profits. When the price is below a set price (such as 10% from your purchase price), use a market order to sell it. When the timing score is the highest, be very cautious as it cannot go any higher, or a peak is close.

Example

Here is an example of how to find the momentum stocks for your portfolio.

Bring up Finviz.com. Select Screener. Select 20-Day Simple Moving Average above 20%. Sort the screened stocks with this parameter. Today I have about 100 stocks.

Limit your selection to fit your requirements and preferences. Here are some sample criteria: U.S. companies only, capital cap over 100 M, price over $2 and relative volume over 1. Ignore ETFs.

Check whether the screened stocks are peaking (say they have appreciated over 100%) and/or overbought (RSI(14) > 65). Check the reasons for recent surges and evaluate whether the momentum would continue or not. Check out any insider purchases at prices close to market prices.

Strategy #4

This is a variation of the described three strategies. I explain it with a step-by-step approach in implementing it using Finviz.com. Bring it up by typing Finviz.com in your browser.

1. Only buy momentum stocks when the market is not risky. When the tide is up, all ships will flow up. Check out my market timing technique. In the simplest way, enter SPY (or any ETF that simulates the market) in Finviz.com. If SMA-20%, SMA-50% and SMA-200% are all positive, most likely the market is not risky. 20% is more important than the other two.

2. Screen. The following are my preferred metrics and you can change them to suite your requirements and risk tolerance.

From Descriptive tab, Select Small (300M to 2B) for Market Cap, Over 100K for Average Volume, Over 2 for Relative Volume, USA for Country and Over $5 for Price. Repeat it for other ranges such as 100M to 4B in the Market Cap. For 100 M market cap, use over $1 for Price; increase the price for larger market cap such as using 'over $2' for 200 M market cap.

3. From Fundamental tab, select Positive in Insider Transaction.

4. From Technical tab, select 10% above SMA-50 in SMA-20 (Simple Moving Average for the last 20 days) and 20% above 200-SMA in SMA-50. If you have too many stocks, reduce the 10% to 8% or less. Change the selection if they are not desirable for you and/or the current market conditions.

   As of 11/07/2016, I have the following 4 stocks: AAOI, BOOT, LC and NILE. They already had good price increases.

5. Click on the selected stocks one by one such as AAOI. From most other metrics, it is not a value stock. The Forward P/E is 16. Hence, it has some value despite the high P/E of 80. All SMA%s are positive which indicate it is trending up.

6. After you bought the stock, use stop loss to limit any losses especially in this risky market. Conservative investors should stay away from risky markets. I would set a 15% stop loss (i.e. sell it via a market order when it loses 15%).

7. Most likely you will not or cannot buy a stock via a discount price when the stock is trending up.

8. Save the screen with a name such as Momentum, so you do not have to reenter the metrics again.

9. Finviz does not provide a historical database. You can run the test every week (or monthly) and write down the results. Only invest with real money when you're comfortable with your tests. If your expected maximum loss is 50%, double your portfolio size as the money you can afford to lose.

10. Making 55% profitable trades could be very profitable.

11. There are many variations and parameters to this strategy such as RSI(14), Double Bottom in Pattern and New High in 52-Week High/Low.

12. If your purchased stock is moving up, review it every month (preferable every week) and set up a trailing stop. To illustrate, when it is up by 20%, set the stop at the current price (not the price you paid for the stock).

3   Herd theory

When the herd makes money, they think they're a genius. The last one to leave the herd will be the fool of all fools such as the last holders of Lehman Brothers, AIG, Bear Sterns, internet stocks in 2000, etc. The biggest fools are the 'value' buyers when these companies were plunging fast. When a specific stock looked great yesterday and it lost 50% today, it 'must' be super good to some. Wrong! Check out why it plunged. It could be missing some important metric, or something is really wrong with the company that did not show up in the research.

The real genius is the one who makes money all the way up, but leaves before the bubble bursts. Even a genius cannot predict the peak and the bottom, but I'll call him/her a genius if s/he is right better than 60% of the time.

Recently dividend growth stocks have the highest premium in the last 30 years. It is a mild bubble when we've many retired, or retiring folks seeking income. However, the bubble will burst when the interest rates rises. At that time, the long-term bonds with low yields will lose.

Dividend stocks will benefit when the interest rates is low. Bond holders would move to dividend stocks from their low-yield bonds. Long-term bonds lose their value when the interest rates rises, and vice versa.

It is the same for the internet bubble in 2000. I did unload most of my tech funds in early April, 2000. The more I read during that time, the more I got scared. It was partly luck and partly 'genius' to move all these sector funds to traditional industries. At that time, they did not have contra ETFs, so cash, money market fund and bonds would be the best choices.

4   Simplest ways to evaluate stocks

Beginners should trade ETFs only. This chapter is for the readers who are ready or getting ready to trade stocks. In general, ETFs are diversified, less volatile than trading stocks. However, stocks offer higher profit but higher risk.

Many stock researches have already been done recently and some are available free of charge. I have no affiliation with Fidelity except I retired from it. You can open an account with them with no balance. Their Equity Summary Score is one of the best indicators; I check out **value** stocks with scores higher than 8. Concentrate on fundamental metrics such as P/E for long-term holds, and momentum metrics for short-term holds. Add criteria to limit the number of screened stocks. Finviz.com is a free screener.

Several sources

The popular ones are Morningstar, Value Line, The Street and Zacks (currently free for rankings of individual stocks). If they are not free, check out whether they are available from your local library. I have 3 simple ways to evaluate stocks starting with the simplest. In addition, read the articles on the selected stocks from Fidelity, Finviz, Seeking Alpha and many other sources for further evaluation.

Fidelity

Select only stocks that have Fidelity's Equity Summary Score 8 or higher. There are tons of information about a stock. Once in a while I did not agree with this score such as SHOP and ZM that scored high in August, 2020. Include the following for your analysis.

A modified stock selection based on a magazine article

Most metrics are available from Finviz except EV/EBITDA.

1. Forward P/E (expected earnings and not based on the last twelve months). It should range from 5 to 15 (10 to 25 for high tech stocks). EV/EBITDA (from Yahoo!Finance) is a better choice as it includes the debts and cash than P/E; it would be more effective if it uses forward earnings. If you do not use EV/EBITDA, ensure Debt/Equity is less than 0.5 except for the debt-intensive industries.

2. ROE (Return of Equity) measures how well the company uses the capital. I prefer stocks with ROE greater than 5%.

3. Volatility. Conservative investors should select stocks with a beta of less than one (i.e., less volatile).

4. Insider Transactions for sales (i.e., negative) should be less than 5%. If it is -5%, most likely the insiders are dumping it.

5. Compare the metrics such as P/E and Debt/Equity to its five-year average and its competitors (available in Fidelity).

6. Momentum. Check out the SMA-50 (actually SMA-50%) and SMA-200. Ideally, they should be positive. SMA-50% is especially important for stocks you do not want to keep for a long time.

7. Check out articles on the stock as some recent events (for example a new lawsuit) have not been included in the metrics.

8. Compare the trend of the sector this stock is in. Under Finviz, enter the related sector ETF.

Summary

The sources are Fidelity (Equity Summary Score and various comparisons), Finviz and Yahoo!Finance (for EV/EBITDA). Value stocks should be held longer.

Category	Score / Metric	Value /Momentum
Score	Fidelity's Equity Summary Score	Both
Value	EV/EBITDA	Value
	P/E cheaper compared to 5-year avg.	Value
	P/E cheaper compared to its sector.	Value
	Insider Purchases	Both
Safety	Debt/Equity	Value
	Compare it to its sector.	Value
Momentum	50-SMA%	Momentum
	200-SMA% (for long term holds).	Value

Articles	Check out latest events	Both
Market	No purchase if market is risky.	Momentum

A simple scoring system using Finviz
Bring up Finviz.com and then enter the stock symbol.

No.	Metric	Good	Bad	Score
1	Forward P/E[1]	Between 2.5 and 12.5, Score = 2	> 50 or < 0, Score = -1	
2	P/ FCF[1]	< 12, Score = 1	>30 or < 0, Score = -1	
3	P/S[1]	< 0.8, Score = 1	< 0, Score = -1	
4	P/ B[1]	< 1, Score = 1	< 0, Score = -1	
	Compare quarter to quarter of last year			
5	Sales Q/Q	> 15%, Score = 1	< 0, Score = -1	
6	EPS Q/Q	> 20%, Score = 1	< 0, Score = -1	
			Grand Score	
	Stock Symbol Date[2]	Current Price	SPY	

Footnote

[1] Negative values for Sales (due to accounting adjustments), Equity and Book are possible but not likely.

[2] The last row is for your information only. SPY is used to measure whether it will beat the market by comparing the return of this stock to the return of SPY.

The Score
Score each metric and sum up all the scores giving the Grand Score. If the Grand Score is 3, the stock passes this scoring system. Even if it is a 2, it still deserves further analysis if you have time. You may want to add scores from other vendors. To illustrate on using Fidelity, add 1 to the score if Fidelity's Equity Summary score is 8 or higher. Monitor the performance after every 6 months or so to see whether this scoring system beats the market.

Very basic advice for beginners
Beginners should stick with U.S. stocks with Market Cap greater than 800 M (million), Debt/Equity less than .25 (25%) except for debt-intensive

industries such as utilities and airlines and Forward P/E between 5 to 20 (25 for high-tech companies). These metrics are all available from Finviz.com, which is free.

Do not have more than 20% of your portfolio in one stock (unless it is an ETF or mutual fund) and do not have more than 30% of your portfolio in one sector.

For more conservative investors, buy non-volatile stocks whose beta (available from Yahoo!Finance) is less than 1. Beta of 1 represents the market (the S&P 500 index). For example, a stock with beta 1.5 statistically fluctuates more than 50% of the market and hence it is very volatile.

Try paper trading to check out your strategy and your skill in trading stocks. If your broker does not provide one, use a spreadsheet to record your trades or check the availability of simulator.investopedia.com.

#Filler: Silence is golden

I am glad I did not give advice to a friend who had to decide whether to take a lump sum payment or an annuity. The correction in March, 2020 would wipe out a lot of his portfolio if he took the lump sum payment. No one would share his profits when the predictions are correct, but the blame if it does not materialize.

It is the same in investing that nothing is certain. With educated guesses, we should have more rights than wrongs especially in the long run.

Section 3: Simple techniques

For starters, just trade ETFs such as SPY (an ETF simulating the market), and you can skip the rest of the book. It only take a few minutes every month. When the market is not plunging, buy or keep SPY (or any ETF that stimulates the market); otherwise sell it. Do the opposite when the market is recovering.

If you have less than $50,000 to invest, just buy ETFs. Improve your investing skills by reading investment articles from this book and your broker's web site. For example, Fidelity has a lot of information for investors.

Subscription to AAII is recommended. When your portfolio grows more than $50,000, invest on a subscription such as Value Line, GuruFocus, Zacks or IBD (more for momentum traders). Initially, use the information for paper trading on value stocks, which is usually available from brokers.

For the long term, knowledge is most important in your investing life and experience comes next. Retail investors have a lot of advantages over fund managers. However, I advise you NOT to be a trader. Hence, you should ignore the 'fabulous' trade systems that claim to be very profitable. Statistically most amateur traders lose money as they cannot compete with experienced, disciplined traders.

1 Quick analysis of ETFs

Evaluate an ETF

ETFs are a basket of stocks according to the market, a specific sector, country or a specific theme.

Yahoo!Finance used to give the P/E of an ETF. Try to get it from ETFdb.com. Enter the symbol of the ETF such as XLU, and then select Valuation. If it is below 15 and above zero, it could be a value ETF. Also, if the current price is lower than its NAV, it is sold at a discount (or premium vice versa). Compare its YTD Return to SPY's.

Alternatively, get similar info from http://www.multpl.com/. In addition, this website provides the following metrics: Shiller P/E, Price/Sales, and Price/Book.

From Finviz.com, enter the ETF symbol. If SMA-20%, SMA-50% and SMA-200% are all positive, most likely the ETF is in an uptrend. To illustrate, SMA-200 is Simple Moving Average for the last 200 trading sessions (no trading on weekends and specific holidays). The percent is how much the stock price of the ETF is above the SMA. If the percent is negative, it means the stock price is below the SMA.

If your average holding period of your stocks is about 50 days, SMA-50% is more appropriate to you.

If RSI(14) > 65, it is probably oversold; if it is < 30, it is probably under-sold (indicating value).

In addition, ensure the ETF's average volume is high (I suggest more than 10,000 shares), the market cap is more than 300 M, and it has low fees. Most popular ETFs have these characteristics. Beginners should avoid leveraged ETFs.

How to determine if the sector has been recovered

It is easier to profit by following the uptrend of an ETF using the above info. It is hard to detect when the bottom of an ETF has been reached. If SMA-20%, SMA-50% and SMA-200% are all positive, most likely the ETF is in an uptrend or it has recovered. It does not always happen as predicted, so use stops to protect your investment.

An example

First, determine whether the market is risky. Most beginners should not invest in a risky market. Advanced investors can bet against the market or a specific sector by buying contra ETFs or puts.

Next, you want to limit the number of sector ETFs by selecting those that are either in an uptrend or hitting bottom (bottom is hard to predict). Personally, I prefer sectors with long-term uptrends (indicated by articles found in many websites including cnnfn.com and Seeking Alpha.

For illustration purposes only for deteriorating market conditions, I would select the following ETFs: SPY (simulating the market based on large companies) and XLP (consumer staples). XLP should perform better than XLY (consumer discretionary) during a recession as those products are the necessities.

Technical indicators such as SMA-50 (Simple Moving Average for the last 50 sessions), SMA-200 and RSI(14) are obtained from Finviz.com and the rest are obtained from Yahoo!Finance.com. After you buy the ETF, use a stop loss to protect your investment. For example, biotech sector moved up for many months until it crashed in 2015. Change the stop loss value every month to protect your gains in this case.

As of 2/5/2016	SPY	XLP (staples)	XLY (discreet.)
Price	190	50	71
NAV	192	50	73
• Technical			
SMA-50	-4%	0%	-7%
SMA-200	-6%	2%	-7%
RSI(14)	44	50	36
Other	Double bottom at $186		
• Fundamental			
P/E	17	20	19
Yield	2.1%	2.5%	1.5%
YTD return	-5%	0.5%	-5%
Net asset	174 B	9 B	10 B

Explanation
- The figures may not be identical among websites due to the dates they are using.
- XLY has the best discount among the 3 ETFs as most investors believe a recession is coming.
- XLP has less down trend among the 3 ETFs as expected.
- XLY is more undersold among the three as expected.
- Double bottom is a technical pattern that indicates the stock would surge upward.
- SPY has a better value according to its P/E.
- XLY's dividend is the least among the three as they have more tech companies in the ETF. They have to plow back the profits to research and development.
- XLP has the best YTD return among the three.
- As long as the asset is above 500 M (200 M for specialized ETFs), it is fine and all three pass this mark.

There are many metrics such as Debt/Equity not readily available from most websites. Many sites list the top holdings of a specific ETF. Just average the metrics of the top ten or so of its stock holdings.

#Filler: Illogical logic

If we do not test for the pandemic, we would have zero increase in this pandemic. Some silly folks buy this argument. What happens to the once-great country?

Filler: The problems of the U.S.

1. Our political system. We waste time arguing between the two parties. There is no long-term planning, as the other party could claim the credit. Same as corporations' CEOs who care about their yearly bonuses.
2. The politicians have to satisfy their voters. Today give them free cash by jacking up the printing press. And ignore the long-term consequences.
3. We have to protect our workers, our environment... Hence, we cannot compete with many countries.
4. We have spent too much on the military and ignore our crumbling infrastructure.
5. Historically no country can rule the world forever.
6. We blame China, but ignore how hard-working Chinese are.

2   An example

This example evaluates RING, a gold miner, using ETFdb and Finviz that are free from the web. The data is from July, 6, 2020.

Bring up ETFdb and enter RING in the search. There is basic info that are important to me: Sector (gold miners), Asset Size (Large-Cap), Issuer (iShares), Inception (Jan. 31, 2012), Expense Ratio (0.39%) and Tax Form (1099).

They fit all my requirements. The expense ratio is higher than most ETFs that simulate an index such as SPY. I try to trade ETFs using Tax Form 1099 in my taxable accounts. The large cap created about 8 years ago by a reputable company is good.

Select "Dividend and Valuation". P/E of 17.39 is fine in a rank of 11 in 27 in a similar group of ETFs. As in my books, I stated it is hard to evaluate miners. I buy this ETF primarily to fight the possibility of inflation and the potential depreciation of USD. The dividend rate of 0.52% (0.70% from Finviz) is in the low range of the scale; it is fine for me as dividend is not my concern.

There is more info from this website. For simplicity, bring up Finviz:
- The short-term trend is up (SMA-20% = 8% and SMA-50% = 7%).
- The long-term trend is up (SMA-200% = 26%).
- It is close to overbought (RSI(14) = 64%; 65% to me is overbought).
- It is -4% from 52-w High. It has performed well from the YTD, Last Year, Last Quarter, Last Month and Last Week.
- It almost doubled in price from mid-March this year.
- Avg. Vol. is fine.

From ETFdb, check the Holding. It has 39 stocks, so it is quite diversified for this industry. The two top holdings are NEM (19%) and ABX (18%), which is listed as GOLD in NYSX. I also consider buying these two stocks in addition to RING. You can estimate the other metrics that are not available by averaging these two stocks. Here is my summary:

STOCK	NEM	GOLD
Forward P/E	20	25
Debt / Share	0.31	0.24
ROE	17%	22%
Sales Q/Q	43%	30%
EPS Q/Q	389%	254%
SMA50	2%	4%
RSI(14)	59%	60%
Insider Trans	-13%	N/A
Fidelity's Equity Summary Score	6.1	6.8

3 Rotate four ETFs

We can beat the market by rotating one ETF that represents the market such as SPY and cash via market timing. Aggressive investors can add SH or PSQ (contra ETFs) to the four to have better returns during market plunges.

During a market uptrend, rotating the following four ETFs could be more profitable than staying with SPY (or any ETF that simulates the market). Be warned that a short-term capital gain in taxable accounts is not treated as favorably as the long-term capital gain; check current tax laws.

The allocation percentages depend on your individual risk tolerance. You can use indexed mutual funds. Compare their expenses and restrictions. Some mutual funds charge you if you withdraw within a specific time period.

Select the best performer of last month (from Seeking Alpha, cnnFn, or one of many ETF/mutual fund sites). Add a contra ETF such as SH to take advantage of a falling market for more aggressive investors. Add sector ETFs to the described four ETFs such as XLY, XLP, XLE, XLF, XLU, IYW, XHB, IYM, OIL and XLU to expand your selection.

ETFs	Money Market	U.S.	International	Bond
Fidelity		Spartan Total Market	Spartan Global Market	Spartan US Bond
Vanguard		Total Stock Market	Total International Market	Total Bond Market
My choice	Fidelity	SPY	Vanguard	Fidelity
Suggest %				
During Market plunge	90%	0%	0%	10%
After plunge	10%	60%	20%	10%

Explanation

- The above are suggestions only. If your broker offers similar ETFs, consider using them.
- Check out any restrictions of the ETFs and commissions.

- 4 ETFs (one actually is a money market fund) are enough for most starters. They are diversified, low-cost and you do not need rebalancing except during a market plunge.
- The percentages are suggestions only. If you are less risk tolerant, allocate more to a money market fund, CD and/or bond ETF.
- Have at least 10% allocated to the money market fund for safety.
- When the market is risky, reduce stock equities (i.e., increase money market and bond allocations).
- The symbols for Fidelity ETFs are FSTMX, FSGDX and FBIDX.
- The symbols for Vanguard ETFs are VTSMX, VGTSX and VBMFX.
- If you are more advanced, use additional sector ETFs to rotate. Also buy long-term bond funds (such as 30-year Treasury) when the interest rate is 10% or more.

#Filler: Where common sense is not common sense

Excessive printing of money is not a long-term solution. Servicing the huge debt weakens our competitiveness. The politicians just want to buy votes today and finance their campaigns. Our next generations have to pay for these huge debts.

#Filler: Cayman Island

Most global corporations are making fun of our tax system. Moving the "headquarter" to low-tax countries such as Cayman Island with a mailbox, a bank account and/or an office that has never been used is a norm. The profitable Boeing has negative tax liability. What a shame!

4 The best strategy

The best-kept secret in investing is to buy a weighted ETF. I use SPY as an example here. This ETF is well diversified as it keeps all 500 stocks in the S&P500 index. The ETF has higher position (in percentage) on stocks with higher market cap. The stocks with higher market caps usually grow the market cap by having good management and good products. The bad stocks are deleted from the index periodically.

The second best-kept secret is using simple market timing as described in this book to reduce the losses in market crashes.

It is very hard to beat this strategy. You do not need any knowledge in investing, and you only spend a few minutes every month to time the market. The market is risky when the metrics show you so such as the price is close to the simple moving average in using SMA-350 method; in this case you time the market more frequently.

Appendix 1 – All my books

- Art of Investing (highly recommended combining most of my books on investing). It has over 500 pages (6*9), double the size of an average investing book. Similar books: Using Fidelity. Using Finviz.
- Sector Rotation: 21 Strategies, Strategies and Shorting Stocks and ETFs have more specific chapters on the topic.
- Using Profitable Investing Sites. Investing Lessons.
- Best stocks for 2022.
- "Nuclear War with China?"
- Books for today's market: Profit from Coming Market Crash.
- The following books are in a series: Finding Profitable Stocks, Market Timing and Scoring Stocks.
- Books on strategies: Trading System, Swing (Rotation + Momentum), ETF Rotation for Couch Potatoes, Momentum, SuperStocks, Dividend, Penny & Micro Stock, and Retiree.
- Books for advance beginners: Be an expert (highly recommended), Introduce, Investing for Beginners, Beat Fund Managers, Profit via ETFs, Buffett, Ideas, Conservative and Top-Down.
- Miscellaneous: Investing Strategies. Buy Low and Sell High. Buy High and sell Higher. Buffettology. Technical Analysis. Trading Stocks.
- Concise Editions and Introduction Editions are available at very low prices and are competitive with books of similar sizes (50 pages) and prices ($3 range).

Most books have paperbacks. Links and offers are subject to change without notice.

Best stocks to buy for 2022

We care about performance only. Not considering dividends and fees, my last three books in this series have beaten the SPY (the market to most) by **110%, 71% and 25%** from the publish date to 07/01/2021. Next book could be on 12/15/2022

Book	Stocks	Return	Ann.	Beat SPY by
Best Book for 2021 2nd Edition	10	20%	52%	110%
Best Book for 2021	4	29%	52%	71%
Best Book to Buy from Aug, 2020	14	42%	45%	25%
Avg.	9	31%	50%	69%

Sector Rotation: 21 Strategies

- On 5/26/2020, I searched for "Sector Rotation" under Amazon's Book. They are listed in the same order except my book Sector Rotation: 21 Strategies.

| Book | Date | Size[1] | Kindle $[1] | Hard $ |

Sector Rotation: 21 Strategies	**05/2020**	**425**	**$9.95**	**$24.95**
Super Sectors	09/2010	289	$26.39	$49.95
Dual Momentum Investing	11/2014	240	$40.40	$42.20
Sector Investing	05/1996	260		$29.94
Sector Trading Strategies	08/2007	164	$26.39	$16.66
The Sector Strategist	03/2012	225	$26.39	$44.96
ETF Rotation	10/2012	125	**$9.95**	**$14.99**
Optimal... Sector Rotation	07/2015	80		$44.07

[1] From Amazon on size and prices as of 5/25/2020.

My book won in all categories except the price for hard copy in one. However, my book won as the lowest cost per page by a wide margin. In addition, as of 5/2020 I bet that no author besides me made over 4 times using sector rotation starting the amount more than his yearly salary then.

- I have **21** strategies in sector rotation while most books have only one. It ranges from simple rotation of a stock ETF and cash for beginners to many advanced strategies for experts. Most other books have one or two strategies.
- Andrew, a contributor on Sector Rotation article at Seeking Alpha, said, "Great stuff, Tony. It's great to meet experienced traders such as yourself. I had a browse through the book and think your method is a little more refined than mine."
- "You have written the book in a way that makes good and logical sense." Bill.
- Do not be fooled by past performances. Just check the recent performance of the top 50 stocks selected by IBD in the last five years. The mediocre result (hopefully it will change) could be due to too many followers and/or there is no evergreen strategy. I seldom heard the fantastic results from the followers of O'Neil, our greatest chartist. The adaptive strategy of this book shows you how to select the most profitable strategy for the current market.
- I switched most (if not all) my sector funds in April, 2000 from technology sectors to traditional sectors (better to money market fund). We can reduce losses by spotting market plunges and the sector trend.

Investing Strategies: Build, Monitor and Execute

It is similar book as Sector Rotation and Shorting Stocks (below), but concentrates in creating, monitoring and executing strategies.
Shorting Stocks and ETFs
Recent performances.

Stocks	Short Date	Close date	Duration	Return	Annualized
ACVA	06/10/21	09/29/21	111	22%	72%
CCL	07/14/21	09/29/21	77	-8%	-36%
CENX	09/17/21	09/29/21	12	3%	105%
CLOV	09/16/21	09/29/21	13	10%	291%
CSPR	09/16/21	09/29/21	13	33%	917%
EOSE	09/15/21	09/29/21	14	10%	261%
MILE	07/22/21	09/29/21	69	53%	279%
NCLH	07/27/21	09/29/21	64	-5%	-27%
REAL	06/04/21	09/29/21	117	22%	68%
UAVS	06/04/21	09/29/21	117	41%	127%
Average	07/30/21	09/29/21	61	18%	206%
RSP	S&P 500			0%	

It is for education purposes and I am not responsible for any errors. As in most parts of this book, commissions, dividends and fees (interest for shorts) are not included, and hence the returns are less than specified. They are real and all trades for the period.

Stocks	Short Date	Close date	Duration	Return	Annualized
BBIG[1]	09/30/21	11/19/21[1]	50	35%	258%
BFLY	09/30/21	11/18/21	49	14%	107%
EOLS	11/10/21	11/17/21	7	10%	523%
FLDM	10/13/21	11/18/21	36	14%	147%
MKFG	10/27/21	11/18/21	22	-9%	-149%
PAVM[1]	10/20/21	11/19/21[1]	30	34%	413%
TSP	10/05/21	11/18/21	44	-11%	-91%
VRM	10/13/21	11/17/21	35	13%	135%
Average	10/14/21	11/18/21	34	13%	168%
RSP	S&P 500			4%	

Appendix 2 – Art of Investing

Art of Investing consisting of 15 books in 1. Besides saving money and your digital shelve space, it gives you quick reference and concentration on the topic you're currently interested in. It covers most investing topics in investing excluding speculative investing such as currency trading and day trading. It has over 500 pages (6*9), about the size of two investing books of average size.

The 15 books

Book No.	Amazon.com
1	Simple techniques
2	Finding Stocks
3	Evaluating Stocks
4	Scoring Stocks
5	Trading Stocks
6	Market Timing
7	Strategies
8	Sector Rotation
9	Insider Trading
10	Penny Stocks & Micro Cap
11	Momentum Investing
12	Dividend Investing
13	Technical Analysis
14	Investing Ideas
15	Buffettology

The book links are subject to change without notice.

"How to be a billionaire" is for beginners and couch potatoes, who can use the advanced features of this book in the simplest and less time-consuming techniques. Most advance users can skip this section unless they want to use some of the short cuts described.

We start with the basic books Finding Stocks, Evaluate Stocks, Trading Stocks and Market Timing. You can select and start with one of the many styles and strategies in investing such as swing trading and top-down strategy. Many tools are described in other books such as ETFs, technical analysis, covered calls and trading plan.

Many books start with "Why" to lure you to read more and are followed by "How" and then the theory behind the book.
If the book you're reading is beneficial to you, imagine how it would with 850 pages.

\# Most readers' comments are on "Debunk the Myths in Investing", which this book is originally based on. As of 2018, I did not know any of the commentators on my books.

"I skipped ahead to his chapter book 14 (of "Complete the Art of Investing"), Investment Advice just to get a feel of his writing style. His research is phenomenal and doesn't overwhelm with big words or catchy "sales-like" tactics.

I truly believe this ordinary man, Mr. Tony Pow, has a gift of explaining his experience as an investor without the bull crap of trying to make you buy his stuff. He seemingly just wants to share his knowledge, tips, and clarity of definitions for the kind of folks like me who want to understand something FIRST before jumping in with emotions of trying to make a boat load of money. I like the technical analysis side he brings.

Mr. Tony Pow talks about hidden gems in his book; well….quite frankly, he is a hidden gem. Thank you and I will also post my comments about this author to my Facebook page!" – JB on this book.

"Excellent book, recommend to all investors… great knowledge. It has fine-tuned my investing strategies… Your book is hard to set aside, as I read it all the time learning good techniques and analysis of stocks, ETF… Since I purchased your book in March, I have underlined, highlighted and placed tabs on top of pages for quick reference." – Aileron on this book.

"Tony, I just finished reading your 2nd edition. It's my pleasure to report that I found it most interesting. You're welcome to use this blurb if you like:

Debunk the Myths in Investing is an all-encompassing look at not only the most salient factors influencing markets and investors, but also a from-the-trenches look at many of the misconceptions and mistakes too many investors make. Reading this book may save not only time and aggravation but money as well!"

Joseph Shaefer, CEO, Stanford Wealth Management LLC.

"Tony, Great work!" from James and Chris, who are portfolio managers.

"'Debunk the Myths in Investing' is a comprehensive book on investing that deals with many aspects of this tense profession in which with a lot of knowledge and a bit of luck (or vice versa) one can greatly benefit…

Therefore 'Debunk the Myths in Investing' is an interesting book that on its 500 pages offer a lot of knowledge related to investing world and many practical advice, so I can recommend its reading if you're interested in this topic."
- Denis Vukosav, Top 500 Reviewers at Amazon.com.

"490 pages (Debunk) of a genius's ranting and hypothesis with various theories throughout, written light-heartedly with ample doses of humor...Yes, the myth of not being able to profitably time the market is BUSTED...

One might ask... Why is he giving away the results of his hard-earned research for only $20? He states that his children are not interested in investing and wants to share his efforts with the world." - Abe Agoda.

"Excellent book, recommend to all investors... great knowledge. It has fine-tuned my investing strategies... Your book is hard to set aside, as I read it all the time learning good techniques and analysis of stocks, ETF... Since I purchased your book in March, I have underlined, highlighted and placed tabs on top of pages for quick reference." - Aileron on this book.

"Great stuff, Tony. It's great to meet experienced traders such as yourself. I had a browse through the book and think your method is a little more refined than mine."
"Your strategy is very rules based and solid. I sometimes envy people who have developed something like this."

Making 50% in one month
I claim to have the best one-month performance ever for recommending 8 or more stocks without using options and leverage. My following return is 57% in a month or 621% annualized. They are slightly different as I calculated the average from the averages of three different accounts. The average buy date is 12/26/18 and the "current date" is 01/28/19.
The performance may not be repeated. I will use the same screen for the coming years and even the expected 10% (or 120% annualized) is very good.

I used the same screen for searching stock candidates. I spent a total of about 20 hours from Dec. 15, 2018 to Jan. 5, 2019.

Stock	Buy Price	Sold or Current Price	Buy date	Sold or Current date	Profit %	Profit % Ann.	Status
CHK	2.13	2.99	01/03/09	01/18/19	40%	982%	Sold
MNK	16.41	21.45	01/03/19	01/25/19	31%	510%	Sold
MNK	16.43	21.45	01/03/19	01/25/19	31%	507%	Sold
NNBR	5.68	8.58	12/26/18	01/28/19	51%	565%	
NNBR	5.72	8.58	12/26/18	01/28/19	66%	727%	
ESTE	4.35	6.45	12/26/18	01/18/19	48%	766%	Sold
LCI	4.61	8.29	12/21/18	01/28/19	80%	767%	
MDR	8.01	9.13	01/08/19	01/28/19	14%	255%	
YRCW	3.29	5.78	12/21/18	01/28/19	76%	727%	
YRCW	3.26	5.78	12/21/18	01/28/19	77%	742%	
ASRT	3.56	4.18	12/26/18	01/28/19	17%	193%	
UTCC	7.13	11.00	12/26/18	01/28/19	54%	600%	
YRCW	2.92	5.78	12/26/18	01/28/19	98%	1083%	

Best one-year return

I claim to have the best-performed article in Seeking Alpha history, an investing site, for recommending 15 or more stocks in one year after the publish date without using options and leverage.

https://seekingalpha.com/article/1095671-amazing-returns-velti-alcatel-lucent-alpha-natural-resources

Your choice for your next book

I was surprised that one told me $25 is a lot for an investing book. It could be less than a taxi cab to the airport attending a seminar, and the time is peanut comparatively.

"Art of investing 2nd Edition" should be your first choice. If you are short-term trading, I recommend "Sector Rotation: 21 Strategies" and "Shorting Stocks /ETFs 2nd Edition". These books together with "Using Fidelity" and "Using Finviz" share many articles.

A new book every Dec. 15 with a July update (not a promise) is my selections on stocks. So far, the returns of the selected stocks are phenomenal. "A nuclear war with China?" is my views on politics.

Appendix 3 - Our window to the investing world

The paperback version of this chapter can be found in the following link.
http://ebmyth.blogspot.com/2013/11/web-sites.html

- **General**
  Wikipedia / Investopedia /Yahoo!Finance / MarketWatch / Cnnfn / Morningstar /CNBC / Bloomberg / WSJ / Barron's / Motley Fool / TheStreet
- **Evaluate stocks**
  Finviz / SeekingAlpha / MSN Money / Zacks / Daily Finance / ADR / Fidelity / Earnings Impact / OpenInsider / NYSE / NASDAQ / SEC / SEC for 10K and 10Q (quarterly) reports required to file for listed stocks in major exchanges.
- **Charts**
  BigCharts / FreeStockCharts / StockCharts /
- **Screens**
  Yahoo!Finance / Finviz / CNBC / Morningstar /
- **Besides stocks**
  123Jump / Hoover's Online / FINRA Bond Market Data / REIT / Commodity Futures / Option Industry
- **Vendors**
  AAII / Zacks / IBD / GuruFocus / VectorVest / Fidelity / Interactive Brokers / Merrill Lynch /
- **Economy.**
  Econday / EcoconStats / Federal Reserve / Economist /
- **Misc.**
  Dow Jones Indices / Russell / Wilshire / IRS / Wikinvest / ETF Database / ETF Trends / Nolo (estate planning) / AARP /

Appendix 4 - ETFs / Mutual Funds

What is an ETF

ETFs have basic differences from mutual funds: 1. Lower management expenses, 2. Trade ETFs same as stocks, and 3. Usually more diversified but not more selective than the related mutual funds such as NOBL vs FRDPX.

The major classifications of ETFs are 1. Simulating an index such as SPY, QQQ and DIA, 2. Simulating a sector such as XLE and SOXX, 3. Simulating an asset class such as GLD and SLV, 4. Simulating a country or a group of countries such as EWC and FXI, 5. Managed by a manager(s) such as ARKK, 6. Betting a market or sector to go down such as SH and PSQ, and 7. Leveraged (not recommended for beginners).

Fidelity: Index ETFs (https://www.fidelity.com/etfs/overview).
Wikipedia on ETF (http://en.wikipedia.org/wiki/Exchange-traded_fund).

List of ETFs
ETF database (Recommended): http://etfdb.com/
ETF Bloomberg: http://www.bloomberg.com/markets/etfs/
ETF Trends: http://www.etftrends.com/
A list of ETFs. Seeking Alpha.
http://etf.stock-encyclopedia.com/category/)
A list of contra ETFs (or bear ETFs)
http://www.tradermike.net/inverse-short-etfs-bearish-etf-funds/
Misc.: ETFGuide, ETFReplay
Fidelity low-cost index funds:
https://www.youtube.com/watch?v=zpKi4_IJvlY
Fidelity Annuity funds with performance data.
http://fundresearch.fidelity.com/annuities/category-performance-annual-total-returns-quarterly/FPRAI?refann=005

Other resources
Most subscription services offer research on ETFs. IBD has a strategy dedicated to ETFs and so does AAII to name a couple.

Seeking Alpha has extensive resources for ETF including an ETF screener and investing ideas. So is ETFdb.

Not all ETFs are created equal

Check their performances and their expenses.

When to use or not to use ETFs

I prefer sector mutual funds in some industries, as they have many bad stocks such as drug industry, banks, miners and insurers. Most mutual funds cannot time the market.

When you believe a sector is heading up (or contra ETF for heading down), but you do not have time to do research on specific stocks, buy an ETF for the sector; it is same for the market.

Half ETF

Taking out half of the stocks that score below the average in an index ETF could beat the same full ETF itself. I call it HETF (half the ETF). You heard it here first. To illustrate, sort the expected P/E (not including stocks with negative earnings) in ascending order and only include the stocks on the first half. Add more fundamental metrics. It will take a few minutes.

Disadvantages of ETFs

- When you have two stocks in a sector ETF one good one and one bad one, the ETF treats them the same. Stock pickers would buy the one that has a better appreciation potential.
- Sometimes the return could be misleading due to stock rotation. To illustrate this, on August 29, 2012, SHLD was replaced by LYB in a sector fund. SHLD was down by 4% and LYB was up by 4% primarily due to the switch. Unless you sell and buy at the right time (which is impossible), your return would not match the ETF's returns due to the replacement.
- Ensure the performance matches the corresponding index; it is hard due to excluding dividends.

Advantages of ETFs

- We have demonstrated that you can beat the market by using market timing. Between 2000 and Nov., 2013, you only exit and reenter the market 3 times and the result is astonishing.
- It is easy to rotate a sector vs. buying/selling all of the stocks in this sector. Rotating a sector is the same as trading a stock.
- The risk is spread out, and your portfolio is diversified especially for a market ETF or buying three or more ETFs in different sectors.
- Periodically the bad stocks in most funds are replaced by better stocks.

- Eliminate the time in researching stocks.

Leveraged ETFs

I do not recommend them. Some are 2x, 3x and even higher. They're too risky for beginners. However, when you are very sure or your tested strategy has very low drawdown, you may want to use them to improve performance. Most leveraged ETFs and contra ETFs have higher fees.

My basic ETF tables

I include some contra ETFs, mutual funds and Fidelity's annuity. Some of these may be interesting to you.

ETFs and funds come and go. Some ideas and classifications are my own interpretation. Refer to ETFdb for updated information. Not responsible for any error. Check out the ETF or fund before you take any action.

Table by market cap:

Category	ETF	Mutual Funds	Fidelity's Annuity	Contra ETF	Alternate
Size:					
Large Cap	DIA	See Blend		DOG	
	SPY			SH	FXAIX VOO
	QQQ			PSQ	FNCMX
	RYH				
Blend	IWD	BEQGX			
Growth	SPYG	FBGRX			FSPGX
Value	SPYV	DOGGX			FLCOX
Dividend	NOBL	FRDPX			
	VYM				
Mid Cap			FNBSC	MYY	
Blend	MDY	VSEQX			
Growth		STDIX			
		BPTRX			
Value		FSMVX			
Small Cap			FPRGC	SBB	FSSNX
Blend	IWM	HDPSX			
Growth		PRDSX			FECGX
Value		SKSEX			FISVX

Micro	IWC				
Multi					
Blend		VDEOX			
Growth		VHCOX			
Value		TCLCX			
Total					FSKAX
Bond					
Long Term (20)	VLV	BTTTX		TBF	
Mid Term (7 – 10)	VCIT	FSTGX			
Short Term (1 – 3 yrs.)	VCSH	THOPX			
Total	BOND	PONDX			
Corp Invest Grade	VCIT	NTHEX			
High Yield (junk)	PHB	SPHIX			
Muni	MUB	Check state			
Special situation					
Buy back	PKW				

Table by sectors:

Sector	ETF	Mutual Funds	Fidelity's Annuity
Banking[1]		FSRBK	
Regional	IAT		
Bio Tech	IBB	FBIOX	
	XBI	Large	
Consumer Dis.	XLY	FSCPX	FVHAC
Consumer Staple	XLP	FDFAX	FCSAC
Finance	KIE	FIDSX	FONNC
	IYF		
Energy	XLE	FSENX	FJLLC
Energy Service		FSESX	
Gold	GLD	FSAGX	
Gold Miner	GDX	VGPMX	
Health Care	IYH	FSPHX	FPDRC

	VHT	VGHCX	
House Builder	ITB	FSHOX	
	ITB	Perform	
Industrial	IYJ	FCYIX	FBALC
Material	VAW	FSDPX	
	IYM		
Oil	USO		
Oil Service	OIH	FSESX	
Oil Exploration	XOP		
Real Estate	VNQ	FRIFX	FFWLC
REIT	VNQ		
Retail	RTH	FSRPX	
	XRT		
Regional bank	KRE	FSRBX	
Semi Conduct	SMH		
Software	XSW	FSCSX	
	IGV		
Technology	XLK	FSPTX	FYENC
	FDN	FBSOX	
		ROGSX	
Telecomm.	VOX	FSTCX	FVTAC
Transport	XTN		
	IYT		
Utilities	XLU	FSUTX	FKMSC
Wireless		FWRLX	

Footnote. [1] Also check Finance.

Table by countries outside the USA:

Country	ETF	Mutual Funds	Fidelity's Annuity	Alternate
Australia	EWA			
Brazil	EWZ			
Canada	EWC	FICDX		
China	FXI	FHKCX		
EAFE	EFA			
Emerging	VWO	FEMEX	FEMAC	FPADX
Europe	VGK	FIEUX		
Global	KXI	PGVFX		
Greece	GREK			
India	INDY	MINDX		
Indonesia	EIDO			
Latin America	ILF	FLATX		

Nordic		FNORX		
Hong Kong	EWH			
Japan	EWJ	FJPNX		
S. Africa	EZA			
S. Korea	EWY	MAKOX		
Singapore	EWS			
Taiwan	EWT			
	TUR			
United Kingdom	EWU			
Foreign:				
Combination				
Intern. Div.	IDV			FTIHX
Small Cap	SCZ			
Value	EFV			
Europe	VGK			

#Filler: Honey, my book can play music.
https://www.youtube.com/watch?v=HxGT5z6d-GA&list=PLMZa6mP7jZ2b1otqG4tfbgZpLEdh6YiNF

It may cut down commercials by casting it to TV.

www.ingramcontent.com/pod-product-compliance
Lightning Source LLC
Chambersburg PA
CBHW050309220526
45465CB00005B/1910